To Love

To Love

Sonia Devi

PARTRIDGE

To order additional copies of this book, contact
Toll Free 800 101 2657 (Singapore)
Toll Free 1 800 81 7340 (Malaysia)
orders.singapore@partridgepublishing.com

www.partridgepublishing.com/singapore

CONTENTS

A special thanks to my mother, Devaki; I couldn't have made it this far without you. I'm always grateful and blessed to have you in my life.

Friends who've helped me throughout this journey; Neha and Sarah, I wouldn't have been able to complete this book without the both of you. Thank you.

Love,
Sonia Devi

"*Love*"

Love is not some
fleeting desire which disappears like
foam,
it's unquestionably life changing.
It's absolute.

"Weaknesses"

I love the simplicity in you,
You make me feel calm,
So very very calm,

Everything seems to be serene,
like the ocean.

It's more of a curse than a blessing,
I need you constantly.

It makes me feel powerless,
no control over my life.

I don't want to be loved for the fragileness
in me.

"*Betrayal*"

I remember our last kiss.
A tender kiss on the forehead.

Odd yet I brushed it off,
We were in love with each other,
I thought.
You weren't…
    …I was.

"A Kiss"

Kiss me hard,
  before you leave.

A kiss that marks my day,
A kiss that I wouldn't forget,
A kiss where the heat can be felt the next
day,
A kiss where I would crave for more,
A kiss that screams that I'm yours,
A kiss where the touch of your lips can
still be felt.
A kiss that lasts even if you're gone to the
afterworld.

"*No*"

How do I get myself out of this mess?

I can't go back to the relationship we had
before,
I won't be able to control myself around you.

"Heart"

My heart -

broken into pieces.
547 days –
to land on serenity.

"Trouble"

You seek me.

Even when I'm not here,
Even though you can't come in like before,

I wouldn't let you,
Yet you still seek me,

Why?
Why trouble yourself?

"My Love"

I miss you

I kept my distance,
I can't, it hurts.
I took the courage to call you,
You answered.

I was delighted.
We talked for hours, it felt like the old days.

It felt good, really good.
I wish I was by your side.
To be able to touch you.
To kiss you.
To be embrace by you.
To be with you till dawn breaks.

At twilight,
   you told me,
      that you're married now.

You took me by surprise,
I thought I was the one,
I thought I was always on your mind,
Wasn't I?

Was I too late?
Or did you make a mistake?

Tell me,
Tell me you were lying,
Tell me your sweet love hasn't died,
Tell me why we had to end?

All those lonely times,
      were you with her?

"*you*"

The moonlight trails my path,
How beautiful...
  ...wasn't I mesmerize by it back then?

I remember –
  you were there, my eyes were on you.

"06"

June –
The month where you wandered into my life
and fed on my soul.
I silently let you go,

Now –
Peace and love feels eternal.

"Dad"

The girl returns home and lies down by her father's coffin.

Not knowing; why?
Are you reaching heaven's gate or
...are you still here?

She wonders.
Tears are shed by others yet she feels nothing.

"*Language*"

Je t'aime
Dhivehi - varah loabi vey
Te iubesc
Mea tum se pyaar karta hu

> words to indicate your love,
> just words,
> merely words to you.

"Time"

I was lost so lost,
Everything seems to be falling apart,
Nothing seems hopeful,
Even the fresh flowers around me seem dull.

I was drifting away from reality,
I slept all day long just so time flies.

No one noticed,
No one to blame,
No one can help me but me.

I just needed time.

Time?
If time could stand still, I'd freeze it here.

"A Call Away"

You understand me even over the phone,

My silence,
My sadness,
Everything.

I can't stop myself from letting you go...
     ...but this has to end, it's intoxicating.
          It's going nowhere.

"*Cry*"

She's almost emaciated yet while her body
is weak,
mentally she's strangely positive.

Don't you want to cry?
Why did we separate in the first place?
I couldn't remember.

"First Sight"

He has such a charismatic smile and a
political acumen.

My first impression of you.

I would never get along with him,
He's so far from my touch.

It feels like oceans between you and me.

I'll be content by just looking at him,
So I thought till he brought his lover.

The truth is I'm gay,
I've been using him as my regular dose of
eye candy,
But it doesn't seem enough.

I wanted more,
I needed more,
I want you.

"Happiness"

It was fun...
    ...was that 'happiness'?

You're gone.
An empty house.

This feelin',
With trash and dirty laundry around,
There's no one here to get mad at me,
Someone...
    ...anyone...
      ...you.

"*Anger*"

Why was he so passionate towards me?
I'm angry,
I don't want to remember.
I don't want to be reminded because when
I do,
I lose control over my body.

It's a vicious cycle.

"*Chaos*"

You left,
Not knowing what else to do
   or
Maybe I was in shock,
I stayed in my room.

I kept living but I'm starting to lose it.
I'm being engulfed by the chaos.

"Believe Me"

Trust -

just as I didn't believe him,
he couldn't trust me either,
just like I was feeling insecure,
he felt the same way.

"*Sorry*"

I thought I was young and foolish.

Years passed, yet I still love you.

I knew you were the one the moment I laid
my eyes on you.
But I was too late...

You were with someone else,
Someone who looks like me,
I was baffled.

Why didn't you tell me?
Why - that you love me,
I would've gave you a chance.

Or was I too blind?
I knew you tried, you were tired weren't you?

I'm sorry.

"Breathe"

Somehow it is easier to breathe when I'm with you. It's too late now.

I've put an end to this troublesome relationship. The pain is just too much to bear. I'd rather end this than live with you another day.

"*Mine*"

I'll make you completely mine.
I want to spend my life by your side,
So give me all of you.

Even the spoiled you.
Your lips,
Your fingers, all of it.

All of it is mine.

"Happy?"

You look so happy now.
I guess this is love.
I feel encircled by your love.

"Ease"

Since the first time we met, she has made
me feel at ease.
I couldn't help but fall for her.
I wanted to stay by her side.
I don't want to lose her,
But it's so,
complicated.

"*Speak*"

Could I ever tell her I love her?

Knowing she was running away from
me was the most painful thing I had to
endure.
Being touched by her in return,
feeling each other yet I hurt her.
I'm the worst.

"Marriage"

Would there ever be a perfect world where we can live without "their" gazes?

I want to be serenity in white when I walk down the aisle.

You stood at the end of the aisle - to hold me and the priest goes...

"Will you have this man to be your husband, to live together in the covenant of marriage?

Will you love him, comfort him, honor and keep him in sickness and in health and forsaking all others, be faithful to him as long as you both shall live?"

Will I ever be able to call you my
husband?
Will you ever be able to call me your
husband?
Will we ever?

"Coward"

Even though he said I'm the only one,
Let's me into his heart,
Until this very day,
I've only run away from his touch like a
coward.

Do I not love him?
Do I not trust him?
Or am I insecure with my own feelings?

"*Bind You*"

The ring,

I'll always wear it,

> you have no idea how happy I
> am whenever I'm with you.

To bind you to me forever, I might
be greedy and merciless when it
comes to loving you; despite that
could you still stand by me?

"*Addiction*"

Like ecstasy...

    ...I was drawn to her.

I hurt her the most when I was high on
drugs, but she stood by me for years.
I abused her.
Now she's gone.
Not to her mom's place.
But from the world.

For that, I'm sorry.

"*Lies*"

Everything you ever said was a lie.
You messed up.
I felt like ripping out every memory, scar
and dirty little secret from that
black heart of yours.

"*Ignorance*"

Ever since that day,
she has been blatantly avoiding me.

It fueled my desire to want her more.
I feel something from the pit of my
stomach whenever you lie.
Anger?
Or disappointment?
I wonder.

"Lust"

I don't need love,
I don't want to get hurt again,
Just lust is enough,
Just satisfying my body's desire.

Something somewhere in my heart is
frozen,
Even I can't melt it.

The me who is frozen beneath,
Probably for the rest of my life, won't melt,
No matter who it is,
No matter who,
Love will never happen.

"Her Face"

Ever since then...

...whenever I close my eyes, the image of her face never seems to leave my mind.

I want to know more about her...

...so much that my eyes have been following her. To feel such a way is a first for me.

"A Wall"

I built a wall between us,
I hate my own cowardice.
Finding a way to distance myself without
hurting anyone and to protect myself; it's
chaotic and scary.

"My Girl"

Do you like her?

Her voice
Her eyes and fingers.
Her gentle movements
I like them all.

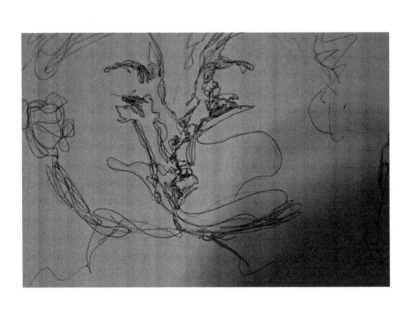

"Trigger"

Her cheeks flush when I tease her,
Her body tenses when I touch her,
She gets embarrassed,
She tries to hide her face,
Her fruitless struggles only manage to
arouse me even more.

"Jump"

I'm tired.

Do I want to jump?

It's tiring...
    ...this cycle of disappointment.

I'm tired,
I can't pretend anymore.

The lies kills me,
It's better to jump...
    ...it hurts less.

The pain will be gone...
    ...gone forever, I would love that.

    Someone,
    anyone...
    ...help.

"Heat"

Whenever she walks by me...
...heat spread from my cheeks and
overflowed inside me.

Like burning fire.

"*Shy*"

She uses her sharp tongue to hide her
embarrassment, she becomes sulky when
she can't talk back.
Adorable.

"Friends?"

In reality we're not friends but...
    ...we're not exactly strangers either.

We've cross paths,
This vague sense of distance.
What are we?

"Smile more"

I wasn't able to smile.
I wasn't able to express.
I wasn't able to be happy.
I wasn't able to laugh.
I wasn't able to love.
I wasn't able to live.
I wasn't able to feel warmth.

You changed that,
You made me feel,
You made me live...
   ....laugh and love....but
most importantly you made me feel warmth.

"Daylight"

'till dawn breaks,
stay.

"Different"

Nobody knows,

Nobody knows that we were in love with
each other. We kept it quiet.
We knew they wouldn't approve.

We wouldn't too if we were strangers.

We weren't,
we were lovers with different
ethnicity.

Ethnicity full of warmth and love.
Why are "they" against us?
Why hate?
We want to love, just love.
Why hold us back?

Even though I love you, it didn't feel
good, it felt like betrayal.
A betrayal of "their" trust.

"Distance"

Distance is so so fragile...

    ...it either kills us or makes us stronger.

"*Where are you ?*"

He's not here today either,
wait,
so what if he was?
What was I expecting?

"Memories"

If only throwing away memories was as easy as deleting your number from my cell.

Countless of sleepless nights thinking of you.

Nothing comes closer to the way I needed you when night fell,
To be able to touch you,
Hug you,
Hear you,
Hold you.

By your side I sleep much better...
...so stay.

"*Touch*"

The way he treated me was profusely hot
and unbearably kind.

"*Emptiness*"

He came straight back to me,
It's stupid how happy that makes me,
Even so,
There's no way I want to feel that same
emptiness ever again.

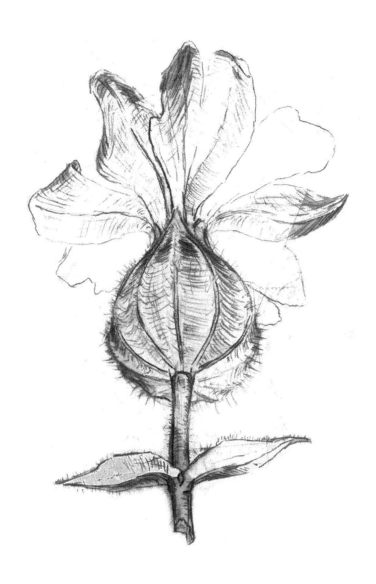

"Easy"

A complicated yet simple story...

...it would have been perfectly natural for this to have been resolved at the beginning. So then why are we running around in circles?

"Desire"

This desire,
that I can't help but want to devour you,
this impulse to suffocate you
must mean
love.

"Fools"

We're so stupid.
We tried to fool ourselves,
With our words,
All we wanted was to be with each other.

"*Sensation*"

Being with you –

it's an intoxicating sensation
that makes me go numb.

"Guilt"

If you love me why did you leave me?

Last night,
The places you touched me so
passionately,
I felt something,
I felt like this was the last time,
Was I wrong?

Something felt odd,
Your eyes,
You never looked at me,
You kept them close,
Those blue eyes that I'm drawn to,
Why did you close them?

Were they full of love?
Or guilt?

Guilt towards your wife?
Guilt towards your children?
Guilt that began this affair?

"Oh Sweet"

Being wanted by the person I love,
gave me more sweet fulfillment
than I could ever have imagined,
to the extent where if I lose all of this,
I wouldn't know what
would become of me.

"Hush!"

Why do you try to protect me?
You never tell me anything and I'm
always...

always left out of the loop.
As time goes by I understand you less and
less.

"We"

Let's…
that will never happen,
even if our paths cross for a second,
we just head off in different
directions the next moment,
every time.

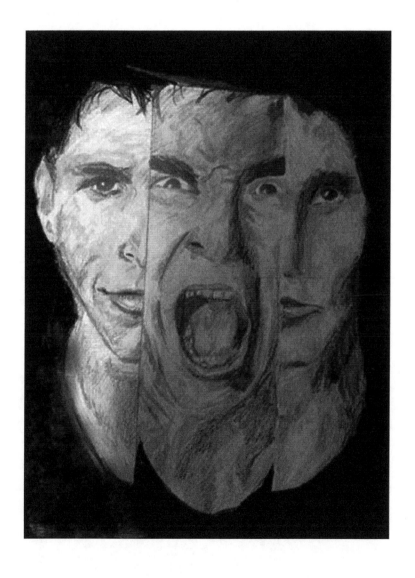

"Mad"

Anger
Purely anger, so don't leave
I promise I'll change.

"Left me"

How blessed am I to have known you?

You may not be blood but you have a
special place in my heart.

How blessed am I to be loved and cared
by you?

So content.

It all came crushing down when you went
out that day.

That rainy day,
You went out to get a pack of cigarettes,
It was chilly,
I was making pancakes while listening to
Birdy.

I was happy,
So so happy,
To know I have you by my side.

But a few hours passed,
I was worried.

The phone rang,
I thought it was you,
I was wrong.

The police called,
You met an accident,
You died instantly.

I stood by the phone in shock,
Speechless.

You kissed me,
You said you'll be back.
You're gone.

You left me,
You left me,
You left me,
.....and the baby.

"Live With Me"

I guess you aren't really serious about living alongside with me.

I am an idiot to hope.

"Hunger"

I'll always continue to hunger for her,
while I know I'll never understand it all,
I guess I'll never be bored either.

"Our Eyes"

This is the first time our eyes have met like this.
Right now...
   ...his eyes are full of me.

"07"

It's been seven long years,
It's time...

   ...I want to hear the words you're afraid
to say out loud. Those three words you
keep hidden in your heart.

Say it.
That is all I want from you, so please say it.

I need to know.

"*Just For Today*"

Days where you treated me kindly,
you gave me the slightest hope in my
wounded heart.

Hope to be loved and not used as a
punching bag.

Yes, we were in love,
I still am but along the way you stopped,
You raised your hand,
I just stood there accepting, it was
dreadful.

He was mad, it's okay.
He will never leave marks on me anymore,
Only today, he was mad.
Just for today, it would be fine.
Just brush it off, you'll be fine.

As expected he loved me...
We went out for dinner, a peck on the
cheek...oh how I missed those...
I'll stay. He still loves me.

I was wrong.
He continued, why ?

"*Love*"

Sometimes I simply love.

Love –
with my entire soul, just too much.

"My love"

Ma -

Someone who believes in me,
My pillar of strength,
My drive,
The one I admire the most.

Love you.

"*Storm*"

The storm will soon pass,
let your heart be softened by my embrace,
don't hate.

"*Not Easy*"

No love is easy.

You knew,
I knew,

We knew...
    we love each other.

But we can't,
      our age difference...we can't,
it's too wide.

We had to depart, no one will ever replace you.

No one.

"*Pain*"

Your insensitivity -

brought pain and fear...

... I need to leave but my voice.

Where has it gone?

"My Person"

You're my Raison D'etre.

"*To Love*"

Is it good?

To love when you felt empty.
To love when you had no one.

To love just to feel.
To love just to move on from another.

To love when I needed you the most.
To love when I was alone.
To love when I love you.

But it was all just a game to you.
Just a game to you.

A rascality move.

"*Lies*"

Such gentle expression he has...

When he lies,
Kills my soul.

"*Baby*"

A baby? Yours?

You impregnated her,
You took advantage of her, while you were
with me.

How could you?
A wimpy quarrel and you seek another
out of anger.

You bear the responsibility with her.
You should but...
    what about us?

"*Him*"

He could never love someone, he won't
love but (he) unfolded his soul.
Open to his true-self.
Finally - the burden he carried flew away.

"*you*"

Sometimes the thought of you,

belies
the fragileness inside me.

"To Feel"

Even if it's just a temporary whim or if she's just playing with him.

Just for now,
it's fine,

He just wants to feel.

"Future"

He fears the future,
He sinks into his darkest thoughts.

The thoughts of them knowing,
the truth of him. The truth - he's
different.
He's gay.

"*Pain*"

Someday you will remember and let go of a long held breath, it will be painful.

A pain like that you've caused me,
A pain that would make you run back to me,
A pain that would destroy your pride,
A pain that would allow you to love me without "their" gazes,
A pain where you'll finally call out my name.

A name that's worth calling out over and over.
A name that you'll love to whisper at night,
A name that you'll grow old with,
A name that you'll be content with by your side for eternity.

"Gone"

This dark aura is surging up.

It irks him.

His entire lifestyle was tightly connected
to her spontaneously.

She's gone.

"*Listen*"

Be close to me,
I'll listen to you.

A voice mixed with honey, whiskey and
smoke - I'll listen.

So come back,
my love.